A Beautiful Day

treasure every moment

40 Devotions

Gwen Ford Faulkenberry

summerside

Summerside Press™
Minneapolis, MN 55337
www.summersidepress.com

A Beautiful Day
© 2011 by Gwen Ford Faulkenberry

ISBN 978-1-60936-229-4

Scripture references are from the following sources: The Holy Bible, King James Version (KJV). The Holy Bible, New International Version®. NIV®. Copyright © 1973, 1978, 1984 by International Bible Society. Used by permission of Zondervan. The New American Standard Version® (NASB). Copyright © 1960, 1962, 1963, 1968, 1971, 1972, 1973, 1975, 1977, 1995 by The Lockman Foundation. Used by permission. The New King James Version (NKJV). Copyright © 1982 by Thomas Nelson, Inc. Used by permission. The Amplified® Bible (AMP). Copyright © 1954, 1958, 1962, 1964, 1965, 1987 by The Lockman Foundation. Used by permission. THE MESSAGE. Copyright © 1993, 1994, 1995, 1996, 2000, 2001, 2002 by Eugene H. Peterson. Used by permission of NavPress, Colorado Springs, CO. The Holy Bible, New Living Translation (NLT), copyright © 1996, 2004. Used by permission of Tyndale House Publishers, Inc. Wheaton, Illinois. *The Living Bible* (TLB) copyright © 1971. Used by permission of Tyndale House Publishers, Inc., Wheaton, Illinois. The New Revised Standard Version (NRSV), copyright 1989, 1995, Division of Christian Education of the National Council of the Churches of Christ in the United States of America. Used by permission. The Revised Standard Version (RSV), copyright 1946, 1952, 1971 by the Division of Christian Education of the National Council of the Churches of Christ in the USA. Used by permission.

Cover, interior layout, and typesetting by Thinkpen Design, Inc. | www.thinkpendesign.com.

Summerside Press™ is an inspirational publisher offering fresh, irresistible books to uplift the heart and engage the mind.

Printed in the U.S.A.

For Stone, my beautiful one

My lover spoke and said to me,
"Arise, my darling,
my beautiful one, and come with me.
See! The winter is past;
the rains are over and gone.
Flowers appear on the earth;
the season of singing has come...."
Song of Solomon 2:10–12 NIV

Contents

Introduction

I typically don't like devotional books. I know there are good ones out there, but many of what we see in today's market are full of fluff. Writers or compilers pull random quotes from some online database, make a cheery comment or two, send the manuscript to a savvy designer, and *bang!*—the world has another pretty book to set on the coffee table to catch dust. What's inside the lovely cover is anticlimactic; the message inside doesn't have much power to change a life.

I seem to be a devotional-book magnet. I suspect a lot of Christian women are. The books usually make affordable gifts, and it seems a nice gesture to give something "spiritual" like that, as we often do at showers and holidays. Most of us have full shelves of these pretty books that we seldom read. I confess I've even regifted a few. But one devotional book came across my desk a couple of years ago that actually did have the power to change my life, which is why I mention it here. The book is *Today Is Your Best Day* by Roy Lessin.

The premise is essentially this: *every day of my life, if I'm a Christian, is my best possible day*. That may not sound so bold if I reflect on the goodness of God, the joys of walking with Him, the blessings that come my way.... But what about the day I lose my job? Someone I love dies? My spouse leaves? Or I find out I have cancer? What about those days? Does anyone have the audacity to claim that those days are also my best days?

Lessin does. He sets forth in very loving, biblical truth that if God is sovereign, which He is, and God is good, which He also is, then every day can be our best day regardless of the circumstances—because God is with us. And He has us right where He wants us to be in order to accomplish His will in us and through us. Personally, I'm edified and inspired by this truth.

Meditating on the sovereign goodness of God since I read Lessin's book has brought me to an interesting place. I find myself looking at life—and thus writing stories—through the lens of a similar premise: if God is sovereign and God is good, then every day can be beautiful. Even the ugly ones.

Days of Grace

Beautiful by Design

"He has sent Me...to give them beauty for ashes...
that He may be glorified." Isaiah 61:1, 3 NKJV

On a recent vacation, I spent extra one-on-one time with Adelaide, our youngest child. While Stone and the others were out in the waves, we'd be out on the beach, building sand castles or strolling for shells, or relaxing inside the house, taking naps.

One day we took a walk along the beach and looked for shells. As Adelaide toddled beside me, I combed the sand with my eyes. I was on a quest to find the perfect specimens to take home to my sister-in-law, who shared my dreams of filling apothecary jars with a potpourri of sand dollars, starfish, conch, scallops, and clams. It was a vision fit for the pages of Pottery Barn.

As Adelaide and I walked, I'd pick up a shell, examine it, and then toss it to the ground if it didn't fit certain specifications. I had precious few in my bucket, while hers overflowed. Soon she started chucking shells into my bucket.

"No, Adelaide," I said, taking out a broken shell, "Mommy doesn't want this in her bucket."

She gave me a puzzled look but kept on walking. In another minute she placed something else in my bucket, which I immediately took out.

"Adelaide, quit putting things in my bucket. You have your own."

I tossed the barnacle-ridden oyster back onto the sand, and Adelaide quickly retrieved it, tucking it under her arm.

She groaned at me in frustration. "Why, Mommy? Why don't you want dese shells?"

I bent down to her level to bestow my infinite wisdom. "Honey, most of these are broken. They're just pieces, or they have ugly spots like this." I showed her the barnacles that had glued themselves to one of her conchs. "Mommy wants the really pretty ones."

She stared at me in perplexity. I could see that she was processing what I'd said and coming to her own conclusion.

She held out her collection. "Dese pretty."

And then, as if the matter were settled, she grabbed a shard of a giant clam and deposited it into my bucket. She proceeded to fill my bucket to the brim with pieces the ocean had spit out onto the sand.

Back at the house, Adelaide dumped out the buckets in order to display our spoils. I gasped. They *were* pretty. And the mix of them together—the bits of broken shells tumbling together as a whole—was exquisite. A work of art.

It occurred to me that those shells are like days in our lives—just pieces, some of which have ugly spots. But when the Lord arranges them together for His glory, the design that emerges is beautiful.

In God's hands, your life has a beautiful purpose. Trust Him today. His grace can take us from ashes to amazing!

Thoughts in Flight

I look up at your macro-skies, dark and enormous,
your handmade sky-jewelry, moon and stars
mounted in their settings. Then I look at my
micro-self and wonder, Why do you bother with us?
PSALM 8:3–4 THE MESSAGE

I love to travel, but I hate to fly. I guess I've got an active imagination. When the plane creaks or the pilot does something to change the wings or there's turbulence or it's time for takeoff or landing, I tend to get scared that something is going wrong. Since 9/11 it's gotten a little worse, because now I sit in my seat and scan the faces and bags of otherwise normal-looking people for signs of terrorism.

On a recent flight, I was with a friend. While I was contemplating the virtues of getting a Valium prescription before my next trip, she seemed quite serene. I asked her, "Do you like to fly?"

She looked out the window beside her and then looked back at me. "Yeah, I do."

"Why? I mean, doesn't it scare you at all?" I chewed on a fingernail.

"Nah. You know, statistics say we're much more likely to die in a car wreck than a plane crash; but anyway, I figure God's will trumps statistics. I'll go when it's my time."

I pondered that.

"You know why I really like flying?" she asked.

"Why?" I couldn't imagine.

"It takes me out of the day-to-day world I live in, where my personal dramas and other people's demands and what's going on around me seem so big and important. I get up here, above all of that, and look down and see that it's pretty small. Flying reminds me of how big God is and that, really, I'm just a speck on a planet that's a part of a great big universe."

I'd never really thought about it that way, but she's right. It's rather humbling. And for that reason, it would probably be healthy if everyone could fly a little bit more—if not in an airplane, just out of our own self-centeredness—to a place where we could be mindful of how small we are and how big God is.

There's also a lot of His beauty in that place. It's the perfect illustration of grace. That great big God looks down and sees us, specks that we are, and He remembers that we are dust. But because of His massive love, we're dust that He died for. And that fills my little, insignificant life with purpose and hope.

Lord, I want to be humble before You. Give me eyes to see Your beauty and wisdom to understand my place in Your design.

The Power of the Cross

*For the message of the cross is foolishness to those
who are perishing, but to us who are being saved it
is the power of God.* 1 CORINTHIANS 1:18 NKJV

My friend Rick Suarez is obsessed with the cross. I know that firsthand because everything he ever talks about is the cross.

He comes by it honestly. The son of a blue-collar worker, Rick became a multimillionaire in his early twenties by selling horoscopes. An atheist, he lived the life of a totally hedonistic king. He messed up his life and his family. After he nearly died from being high on drugs and alcohol and wrecking his Porsche, God got his attention. He surrendered his life to the Lord, got rid of the horoscope business, built a new fitness-equipment empire, and went on to rebuild his family while being very active in church.

It would seem for some that the story should have its happy ending there. A + B = C is the economy of some belief systems; once Rick turned everything over to the Lord, he should have been blessed in every way and have no problems. That has not been the case. You can read the whole story in Rick's book, *The Lost Secret*. But suffice it to say that just as he was doing all of the right things and everything outward seemed to be perfect and blessed, Rick was dealt a blow that would rock his world, destroy his health, and strip him of his identity as a "good Christian businessman."

"It was about that time I began to learn that A plus B doesn't always equal C in God's economy," Rick said with a laugh. "Works-based salvation, the idea that I have a right to expect certain things from God, the belief that what I do makes Him love me more or less, even my concept of the church and its role in society— all of it was put to death at the cross."

As with any death in the kingdom of God, there would be a resurrection. Rick's health returned, and although he lost his business, spiritually he has gained so much more. "I got more of Jesus," he told me, with tears streaming down his face. "And every day I go deeper into His grace."

Recognizing that we must die to self again and again in order to know more of Him, Rick now lives out his faith in its simplest form: "It's all about Jesus. Everything goes back to the cross."

Jesus, I'm willing to go to the cross with You. I choose to die to self so that I might gain more of Your beauty.

Free at Last

He hath sent me to bind up the brokenhearted, to proclaim liberty to the captives, and the opening of the prison to them that are bound. ISAIAH 61:1 KJV

Euna Lee and Laura Ling, reporters for the American Current TV channel, had been in captivity for 140 days when a North Korean prison guard summoned them. Fearing the worst, they believed they were about to be sent to a labor camp to begin their sentences.

After supposedly crossing the border from China without entry permits, the women were arrested and tried by Kim Jong Il's regime. Their punishment would be twelve years in a camp where former inmates claim to have been starved to the point of eating rats and earthworms and describing such torture as being hung by the wrists or confined for weeks in a cell too small to stand up or lie down in.

But instead of going to this labor camp, the two women were led into a room where Bill Clinton, a former U.S. president, was waiting. "We were shocked," said Ms. Ling through sobs, "but we knew instantly in our hearts that the nightmare of our lives was coming to an end."

When I heard the story of this rescue mission, I was so happy for these women. After five months in prison and the dread of twelve years of North Korean hell, they were flown home to the cheers of a nation and the love of their families, which, for Lee, included a four-year-old daughter. Bill Clinton was billed by some as a modern knight in shining armor.

It's a good illustration for the gospel. Captive in the prison of human flesh, we're bound by our own propensity to sin. There would be no hope for our condition except that Jesus loved us and came to save us. But sometimes we seem to forget that what happens at salvation keeps happening for the rest of the Christian story. He keeps on coming to save us whenever we need bailing out.

You might say we live in enemy territory. As Christians we tend to push the boundaries—or just find ourselves near them—and end up in prison. A prison with multiple rooms. In my thirty-seven years, I've done time in the cells of pride, guilt, and doubt, to name a few. There are rooms for everything evil under the sun: disappointment, fear, anger, confusion, illness, depression, and even death. Whatever is the evil and wherever we are, no matter how low, Jesus meets us there. He's the only One who has gone the distance of the grave and conquered it, and He did that to save us... not only for eternity, but in the here and now.

You weren't meant to live in a prison. Neither was I. By His grace, the cell doors stand open. He will give you the courage to run through them and into His loving arms.

What do you need to be delivered from today? No matter how strong your captor, Jesus is greater. He has come to set you free.

The Bird
with the Broken Wing

"*And I will bring [them] through the fire, refine them as silver is refined, and test them as gold is tested. They will call on My name, and I will answer them; I will say, 'They are My people,' and they will say, 'The LORD is my God.'*" ZECHARIAH 13:9 NASB

My earliest memories of church are beautiful, and a big part of the reason is a special family, the Laws. Brother Law is the first pastor I remember, and what I remember most about him is that he loved me. He baptized me when I was in the first grade...and there were tears in his eyes when he brought me up out of the water.

His wife, Eleanor, was my teacher at school. She was a magical sort of teacher who would take us outside under the trees and read books to us and let us do things like stand up in front of the class and sing. I looked forward to seeing her every day at school—

and also on Sundays. Barry, their youngest son, was a friend of mine.

Once I was invited to the Laws' home. Although I enjoyed it all, I mostly remember Brother Law showing us his dialysis machine. He let me feel the big cow vein a surgeon had put in his arm when his own became unusable. It stuck out unnaturally and felt like a PVC pipe, only squishier. When he died the town mourned, because he was a hero to all of us, a true follower of Jesus. His family soldiered on in beauty and dignity.

Fast-forward many years to where I'm sitting in a different church sanctuary, listening to Barry Law sing. He's just been through the hardest year of his life, nearly dying of the same kidney disease that killed his father. Now he's healthy enough to be on the kidney transplant list and has come to bless us with a little concert. His wife accompanies him on the piano, and his mother is in the audience.

As Barry makes jokes in his gentle way, the ministry is already beginning. I feel myself being carried a few steps closer to heaven. And when he opens his mouth to sing, I am in the very throne room of God. My heart takes flight and worships.

When Barry sings "His Eye Is on the Sparrow," it comes from a place so raw that I cannot doubt God's care. When we hear "How Majestic Is Your Name," I wonder why I'm ever angry with the Lord or unable to praise His name. And when Barry sings "How Great Thou Art," my spirit says, "Yes! Lord, You are!"

Sometimes faith gets tested so severely that it comes out as pure gold and shines brightly enough for the rest of the world to see. Sometimes, by God's grace, the bird with the broken wing has the most beautiful song.

In what ways is your faith being refined? Ask the Lord to take something ugly in your life today and turn it into a song.

Leaning on the Everlasting Arms

You've kept track of my every toss and turn
through the sleepless nights, each tear entered
in your ledger, each ache written in your book.
PSALM 56:8 THE MESSAGE

The eternal God is thy refuge, and underneath are
the everlasting arms. DEUTERONOMY 33:27 KJV

My friend Garry Clubb's story of grace and hope in the midst of great personal loss speaks deeply to the heart of this book. He has kindly agreed to share his story here:

When Gwen, the love of my life, lost her battle with pancreatic cancer, I was devastated. The overwhelming agony I felt came not only through her passing but also because of the terrible suffering and loss of dignity she endured toward the end. I struggled through each day, my mind filled with a dark, lonely sadness—a depression—that I can find no words to describe. I sought an end to the terrible pain I felt.

You would have had to know my wife to fully understand why. She never had an unkind thing to say and was gifted at reaching out to those who were hurting with a soft touch and an encouraging word. During the sixteen months between the diagnosis of cancer and her death, I never once heard her complain about having cancer or ask why God seemingly was not answering our prayers.

During Gwen's illness, I stayed positive and truly believed that she would be healed, although I was aware of the high mortality rate of those with pancreatic cancer. I looked for the very best treatment available, and we spent time at a cancer specialty center in Houston, receiving great care. The heavens were filled with prayers for Gwen's recovery. Our church, as well as several others, interceded for us constantly. Surely, I thought, with all of those people praying for Gwen's healing, God would hear and heal her. But that is not what

He chose to do. I do not pretend to understand why.

It's been two years now, and though the pain of Gwen's passing has eased only a little, I know that I am not alone. One way God reminds me of His love is through a little country church, where I am able to share in the joy of fellowship and praise Him for His grace and mercy. God never intended me to bear such grief alone. "Praise be to the Lord, to God our Savior, who daily bears our burdens," Psalm 68:19 (NIV) says. Slowly I am learning to give it over to Him, to trust in His sovereignty, to hope again. I am still healing, but my burden feels blessedly lighter the more I lean on His everlasting arms.

What is the hardest thing you've ever been through? Jesus' arms are there for you to lean on, too. The beauty of hope and His grace are yours, no matter how ugly the circumstances.

Days of Faith

A Little Child's Gospel

Truly I tell you, whoever does not receive and
accept and welcome the kingdom of God like a little
child [does] positively shall not enter it at all.

MARK 10:15 AMP

It was a special Sunday for our family. My brother Jim baptized his oldest daughter, Madeline, then five years old.

Hand-in-hand, they stepped into the baptistery at the front of the church, and Madeline looked even tinier than usual, next to her six-foot-five father. He was dressed in a billowing white robe, and she wore a pink T-shirt and shorts. Her big blue eyes scanned the crowd, and she smiled at each member of our church family. She didn't seem nervous, but rather full of Peter Pan–like adventure. When her gaze rested on me, she seemed to shimmer all over with delight. I gave her a thumbs-up.

My brother asked her age-old questions. "Do you believe that Jesus is the son of God?" Madeline answered yes. "Do you believe He loves you so much that He died for your sins?" Yes again. "Do you believe He was buried and raised on the third day?" "Have you asked Him to come into your life and save you?" "Do you believe He has done that?" Yes, yes, yes.

Yes. The word rolled effortlessly off her tongue, and her eyes seemed to exude a trust that was just that easy. *Yes, Lord. I believe.*

As I watched her blond hair bubble under the water and the smile that broke forth across her face when she emerged, I had to catch my own breath. It seemed as if the sun had risen in her eyes. *This is it,* I thought. *The kingdom of God belongs to such as these.*

Too often my grown-up questions keep me from being childlike. I complicate my faith with things I can't explain, things that make me angry or leave me intellectually frustrated. Sometimes these things seem to matter so much, and I give them time and energy that eventually lead to confusion. But when I remember the look in Madeline's eyes that day when she came up out of the water, clarity returns. My questions are overcome by the pure, simple gospel, distilled to a form that a child can comprehend. Jesus, the Son of God, died for me because He loves me. I believe this, and His love saved my life.

Father, create in me a pure heart that trusts You and depends on You for everything, just like a little child.

What Faith Isn't

Now faith is the substance of things hoped for, the evidence of things not seen. HEBREWS 11:1 KJV

People have a tendency to want to put things in neat little boxes. We do this with ideas like faith because it's easier to feel that we're using the concepts appropriately when we can contain them and match them to situations—like we would shoes to an outfit.

The problem with faith is that it can't be contained in a box. It won't fit. Like God Himself, it's way, way too big for us to fully understand. There are great verses that give us clues, like the one above, but when it comes down to it, faith is messy.

I once took a "leap of faith," which meant to me, at the time, that I was trusting God by venturing out into the great unknown. I had lost my job, my husband had quit his, and we believed that God had something wonderful in store. There was a sense of complete abandon as we waited, evaluating each new option as it came to

us on the basis of whether or not it felt like a "calling."
At the end of a few months, a door or two had been
shut in our faces, and we'd passed up a few good
opportunities, still had little direction, and were running out of money. We ended up moving close to
my family and opening a business, which was much
less than the spiritually exciting thing we thought God
had in store for us. Truth be told, it was an act of
desperation.

I look back now and marvel at God's patience. He
continued to bless us, of course, but we also went
through a lot of junk. And though I believe the Lord
used the move and that whole season in order to get us
where He wanted us to go, I no longer see it as a leap of
faith. I see it as crazy—and what's worse, presumptive.

Faith isn't something we create, determine, or plan.
And it definitely isn't something we can mold to fit
our desires. It's a decision, yes, to trust God. Even the
ability to make that decision comes to us through grace.
But beyond that decision, we give up all of our rights to
the outcome. God doesn't have to perform a certain way
to prove His faithfulness. He's God. We can't assume

we know what He's doing. We can boldly ask Him by faith for what we want—but at the same time we give up our rights to it, trusting in His goodness and trusting that He knows best.

In what ways does your faith need to come out of the box?

Tenacious Faith

"Though He slay me, yet will I trust Him."

JOB 13:15 NKJV

One of my best friends growing up was (and still is) Lori Johnston. We went to school and church together and liked a lot of the same boys, clothes, and music, but the thing we had most in common was our family life.

Lori's parents and my parents were friends. They all believed family was the most important thing besides God. Our moms were both stay-at-home moms and then teachers; and our dads, though they had different jobs, were both big on hard work. Lori and I were some of the few kids in school who actually hung out with our siblings. We did this because we'd been taught that siblings are best friends.

Of all of the men in the world who are not related to me—and I've been blessed to have several godly men in my life—I believe that Lori's father, Larry

Johnston, is the one who had the biggest impact on my early character.

On what I know was the worst day of his life, I witnessed something I will never forget. It is engraved on my soul forever.

We'd just been told that John Johnston, Larry's son and Lori's brother, was killed in a wreck. Lori's parents were out of town, so my mom and I sped over to be with my friend and her sister until the others arrived. When Larry and Mary Johnston drove up, Larry emerged from the car looking like a bruised eagle. The girls rushed to him and their mother, and his arms outstretched like wings around his family, gathering them ever closer and closer to himself. From outside the huddle I heard sobs and gasps, and above it all his voice rose, declaring, resolving, crying out to God: "The Lord gave; the Lord has taken away; blessed be the name of the Lord!"

Was I hearing him right? But it was unmistakable. I couldn't get my head around it, but something beautiful I didn't understand resonated in my heart—a tenacious faith. It was the darkest day I could imagine for them. But as I watched the grief, I saw a light flickering, reaching up through the terrible abyss, and overcoming the darkness. I'd never been in this place before.

In the days that followed, there were questions, doubts, and very real pain that on some level would never go away. But as I watched Larry lead his family through that time, I learned a profound spiritual lesson that I would carry with me for the rest of my life: faith stares death and all of its ugliness in the face and yet still believes in the beauty of a Life we cannot see.

Lord, I choose faith today. I choose the beauty of a Life I cannot always see.

Walking by Faith

We live by faith, not by sight.
2 CORINTHIANS 5:7 NIV

It began like any other day in their two years of marriage. Keith went to his job on an exclusive woodsman's property, where he did everything from building fence to operating heavy machinery. He worked with a team of men who were developing over three thousand acres of sportsman's paradise. Sheila was visiting her aunt when her mother called.

"There's been an accident, and Keith may have broken his leg."

Sheila rushed to the hospital, arriving just as Keith did. His unearthly screams as he was moved told her that something was very badly wrong.

"Don't look at my leg," he pleaded when she got to his side. "I may not ever be the same—I may not ever be a complete husband to you again."

"I don't care about that, just as long as you're here!"

The grisly details and the consequences of Keith's accident unfolded in the days and weeks to come. He was running a street sweeper when the brush got jammed with leaves. As the huge machine turned over on its side, Keith's leg was pinned underneath the cab and totally crushed by its weight. Lying there bleeding, he scratched a message into the paint of the cab in case he died before being rescued: *Tell my wife I love her.*

With Sheila at his side, Keith would spend four years healing. There were many surgeries and months in the hospital, and at one point a doctor said that Keith would lose his leg. But God worked a miracle in his life, saving his leg and allowing him to walk again. Amazingly, they never asked why the accident happened. "The question just never occurred to us," Sheila confessed.

Through it all, they lived under a powerful covering of grace, believing by faith that God was working all things together for good. And even though they'll never fully understand the mystery of His ways, one thing they've seen is that God uses their story to minister to others. "When He does that," Sheila said, "we get a little glimpse of His redemptive purpose."

A special opportunity came a few years after the experience, when Keith became the youth director at his church. He gave his testimony, talking a lot about the accident and how God healed him. His niece Lindsay was in the crowd listening. No one but the Lord knew that just days later Lindsay would find out she had a debilitating disease. And He has since used Keith's example as one of the sustaining forces in *her* faith journey, which is a whole other story....

What's the worst day you've ever had? God can turn even our worst days into something beautiful that will bless others.

He's Still Working

*I am crucified with Christ: nevertheless I live; yet
not I, but Christ liveth in me: and the life which I
now live in the flesh I live by the faith of the Son
of God, who loved me, and gave Himself for me.*

GALATIANS 2:20 KJV

I met Lindsay when she was a little girl; my husband
and I started attending church where she went. On
the first Sunday we were there, she did the special
music, bouncing up onto the stage and belting out
"He's Still Workin' on Me." With her big brown eyes
and beaming smile, she brought down the house. She
was simply adorable.

Several years later, Lindsay came home from bas-
ketball practice complaining of a pulled muscle in her
hip. When the pain was still there after a few weeks,
she went to the doctor and was immediately referred
to Children's Hospital. After testing, it was determined
that Lindsay had idiopathic chondrolysis, a disease

with no known cause and no cure. The doctor said there were only fifteen cases documented in the United States and that out of those, only one person had walked after diagnosis. Lindsay went home in a wheelchair.

"My heart was broken," she recalled, "and I cried and cried. I was terrified at the odds, wondering if there was any way I would be able to walk again or have a normal life."

But as her church family rallied around her, her perspective began to change. "I drew strength from the love of other Christians," Lindsay told me. "And as I thought about Keith's testimony, I began to have hope. I thought, *If he can go through something like this, so can I. God had a plan for Keith, and He must have a plan for me.*"

She continued, "I started to realize that this problem was part of a bigger picture. I know it was the result of prayer, but I had a peace that God was with me no matter what happened. And even if I never walked again, I would praise Him from my seat."

Apparently that wasn't part of God's plan, because after five months in a wheelchair, Lindsay went back for a physical exam. All of the tests showed her hip condition to be in remission, and she was released to walk again.

As an effect of the disease, Lindsay now deals with severe rheumatoid arthritis in every joint of her body. But she doesn't allow it to get her down. Now age fifteen, she relays, "I'm kind of glad it happened. If it hadn't, I don't know that I'd be as strong in my faith. And I wouldn't trade my relationship with Jesus for anything."

God's purpose—even in our pain—is part of a bigger and ultimately beautiful picture.

Nothing More, Nothing Less

You have everything when you have Christ.

COLOSSIANS 2:10 TLB

When I was in college, I was a part of the honors program, which provided me with the greatest challenges I had ever faced academically and, on some levels, spiritually. While I had wrestled with God before, it was always within a friendly environment, i.e., asking my own questions and getting help with them from parents, teachers, and friends who were believers. But through the Honors College I met ideas and people who made me feel ignorant, and they demanded that I engage with them.

I remember reading *The Religions of Man* in one class and being impressed by how eloquently the author, Huston Smith, and my professor were able to explain religions such as Buddhism, Hinduism, and Islam.

Some people in the class came to crises points with their own faith after encountering the other options. I never went that far, but I did become frustrated with my lack of ability to explain why I was a Christian.

The professor—whom I adore to this day—grilled me. "What do you believe?" he would ask, and I would answer with some abridged version of the Apostles' or Nicene Creed. "Why?" he would demand in front of the class. I would say something like, "Because, um, the Bible and my experience tell me so." What followed were hard questions about why I believed the Bible, did I think Jesus was God, had I read *The Origin of Species*, etc.—all in an effort not to take away my faith but to make me examine it, articulate it, and eventually own it. Dr. Schedler was not the antichrist some made him out to be. He was a friend who expected you to use your brain as well as your heart and didn't see them as mutually exclusive.

My parents liked my professor and took his methods with a grain of salt. One weekend when I was telling my dad about the class, I expressed my feeling of inadequacy in not being able to explain my beliefs. "No matter how much I know, there's always something to question or doubt," I said.

My dad smiled. "I'm proud of you for researching everything," he responded, "but in the end, being a Christian is not really about knowing, at least not in the intellectual sense. The next time your teacher asks you about your faith, you tell him this—" And then he started singing: "My hope is built on nothing less than Jesus' blood and righteousness."

I've found my dad's advice to be useful for more than answering someone about my faith. This distilled version of Christianity is the most potent, the most satisfying...even when my own heart is the skeptic. My favorite DaySpring card captures it this way: "When you get down to it, the only thing that really matters is Jesus."

Lord, sometimes other things seem so important, but You are the One who satisfies my soul. Help me to see with eyes of simple faith today.

Days of Love

Kierkegaard's Challenge

*Therefore be imitators of God as dear children.
And walk in love, as Christ also has loved us and
given Himself for us.* EPHESIANS 5:1–2 NKJV

Awhile back my husband bought me a copy of *The Essential Kierkegaard*, and even though it breaks my brain to read it, I love it. It affirms me in the truth that, contrary to what many of my brilliant, progressive friends in academia say, you do not have to be stupid to believe in God. And when I read it, I find nuggets of wisdom to write down, in hopes that constant exposure will ingrain them on my soul.

Here's a gem I mined just the other day from his essay entitled "Practice in Christianity":

> Lord Jesus Christ, you did not come to the world
> to be served and thus not to be admired either, or in
> that sense worshipped. You yourself were the way and
> the life—and you have asked only for imitators. If we

have dozed off in this infatuation, wake us up, rescue us from this error of wanting to admire you or adoringly admire you instead of wanting to follow you and be like you (378).

When I read this, it pierced my heart. I'd been in a church service that day, and during the offering I'd played a song on the piano called "I Could Sing of Your Love Forever." While I was playing, I felt an anointing come over my fingers; they just glided over the keys while my heart soared. People sang along, and in that moment we were caught up in the wonder of Him—who He is, how He loves, and the joy of it all.

It was a true worship experience, I'm sure of that. And I know He inhabits those times. But I don't think it was a coincidence that I came home and read Kierkegaard's admonition. See, while it's relatively easy for me to admire Jesus—I could sing of His love forever—it's a whole other issue to imitate Him. And while I'm sure that five minutes of praise mean a lot to Him, Kierkegaard reminded me that a life of worship through imitation means a whole lot more.

How does one follow Jesus and imitate Him? For me it means hard stuff like getting up from that piano bench and loving others around me with an uncritical spirit. Coming home and serving my family, being patient with little ones because He was, reaching out to the sick because He did. Not being too prideful for a menial task. Laying down my life for my friends.

Singing of His love in worship is an offering of praise...but like any offering, it's not worth much unless I live the love I'm singing about.

O Jesus, rescue us from this error of wanting to adoringly admire You instead of wanting to follow You and be like You.

A Shark Tale

For in Him we live.

ACTS 17:28 KJV

With kids eight, six, and two years old, we decided to take a family vacation to the beach. After driving fourteen hours in a minivan (aka sardine can), we finally arrived at our destination. Too excited to check into our house first, the five of us popped out of that van and headed straight for the water. Reveling in the feel of sand between our toes and the sound of breaking waves, it took us a moment to realize that the beach was strewn with baby sharks. My son, Harper, picked up a few, examined their dull eyes and limp bodies, and assessed that they were dead.

While the kids and Stone played at the edge of the water, I asked a woman holding a seining net what had happened to the sharks. "Oh, those are just bait sharks," she said matter-of-factly. "Most likely they're dead because of us." She pointed to the person at the other end of the net, out in the water.

As I pondered the irony of this—and perhaps of the fact that I was feeling sympathy for sharks—I noticed Adelaide. She was making her way down the beach, stopping at each dead shark. With her chubby two-year-old hands, she picked up one and then another, hurling each into the water.

I followed her at a careful distance. "What are you doing?"

She picked up a shark and waved it at me. "I haffa save the baby sharks."

I was instantly reminded of the starfish story, the one everybody tells about the boy on a beach where thousands of starfish have washed up to die. A cynical man walks by and tells him that his efforts won't matter, but the boy throws one starfish after another into the water, saving as many as he can.

People tell that story to inspire others to make a difference, and the starfish actually would have a chance if someone just helped them get back into the water. But Adelaide's sharks were already dead. There was no hope in the world for them.

As I watched my daughter, I sensed that I was seeing a picture of God's love. Sometimes we're really no different than those sharks—spiritually dead and beyond all hope, cast aside on the shore of the world. But the Father looks down at our shriveled forms and sees hope. He assesses our value and finds something He wants—something He loves. And when He reaches down and picks us up, He does something no one else can do. His love brings us to life.

You are valuable to the Lord, and He will never give up on you.

Fill My Cup, Lord

I will pour out my spirit unto you, I will make known my words unto you. PROVERBS 1:23 KJV

I like to read Amy Carmichael when I have quiet time to think. It takes me a long time to get through one of her books, though, because I have to chew on her words like a cow chews its cud. A lot of times I read something she says and just don't get it. Sometimes I don't get it because I don't want to; if I really take the words to heart, they might require something of me that is hard to give. Such was the case with a quote of hers I recently read: "A cup of sweet water cannot spill out bitterness, no matter how rudely it is over-turned." Like many of her sayings, I find this to be terribly challenging.

Most of the time, if my cup gets spilled by accident— if I'm interrupted by an innocent person or otherwise affected by an innocent mistake—my water can be pretty sweet. At least I hope so. I truly try to be patient and kind. But what about those other situations—the not-so-innocent ones? What about the person who knocks me down on purpose? Or perhaps worse, what about the person who has no regard for my cup whatsoever and just plows right over it, breaking it into pieces?

It's in those situations that Carmichael's claim becomes trickiest. I'm very sorry to say that many times I operate under the delusion that my cup holds sweet, pure water, only to find, after it is rudely overturned, that it's full of bitter tea leaves like hurt, anger, or pride.

What is the solution? It's easy to think, when our cup spews bitterness, it's okay in that situation because the other person deserves it. We're under duress. They push us to the point of hurt or anger, and we have no option but to respond as such. Excuses abound. But the truth is, we do have another option. We can choose to respond in love.

Responding to rudeness with love is not easy, and it is not something we can do in our own strength. But the offer comes to us to "be filled with the Spirit" (Ephesians 5:18). The Lord, who understands our dilemma, offers to empty us of our bitterness and fill us up with His love. It is when our cup is overflowing with Jesus that we'll spill out His love on others, no matter what.

What's in your cup today? Ask Jesus to "fill 'er up" with His Spirit.

A Rejection Letter

> *"I am with you always,
> even to the end of the world."*
> MATTHEW 28:20 TLB

I received a rejection letter today, and—though I know it is not—in this moment it feels like the end of the world.

Though there are variations, a typical writing gig goes like this: you come up with an idea for a book, develop that idea into a proposal, and send it out either through your agent or directly to an editor at a publishing house. The editor reads it, and if he or she likes it, it is presented it to a publishing board and either accepted or rejected (or perhaps sometimes shelved for future use). Acceptance means a contract. Rejection means you have to start the process over, if you can muster the confidence.

I actually sent in a few proposals to one place. I had it all planned. I really liked my ideas and had made friends with the characters in my stories. Their lives were starting to take shape in my mind. I could see how people would love to read these books—they'd be entertained and hopefully intellectually and spiritually challenged. Furthermore, if two or three of my proposals were accepted, I'd have secure work for the next season and even a little bit of financial leeway. It was going to be great.

When my editor's name popped up in my inbox this morning, my heart started to beat faster. After months of waiting to hear the good news, the moment had finally arrived!

Dear Gwen,

Thank you for sending in your proposals. Your story ideas are truly delightful, but I am sorry to say that at this time none of them fit our current publishing needs.

Thank you for your interest.
Sincerely,

Sincerely. With just a few polite words, my hopes and dreams for the characters I'd imagined were shot down. Maybe they weren't that interesting after all, and maybe we shouldn't be friends. Maybe their stories would never be told because nobody would want to read them. Maybe I wasn't a good writer after all. Like air going out of a balloon, the characters in my head started fading away. I felt like crying.

Now, I've walked this road enough times with the Lord that I know: for every death we face, there's a resurrection just around the corner. Faith tells me that man—and his rejection or acceptance of my performance—will not have the last word. But since I'm not feeling so strong at this moment, and since I need to be reassured, I'm going to curl up in my Father's lap and let Him love on me for a while. I'm going to believe that He is with me, just the same as in my finer moments—and even to the end of the world.

Go ahead, let Him love on you, too. You'll be glad you did.

God Loves Ugly

"God sees not as man sees, for man looks at the out-ward appearance, but the LORD looks at the heart."

1 SAMUEL 16:7 NASB

I teach writing and literature at a local college. A recent composition class I taught included people from ages nineteen to fifty, with very diverse backgrounds. It was a lively bunch, one I knew from the first day that I would enjoy.

There was one student, though, who puzzled me. His was a small, quiet presence as he came in day after day with his head down before sitting in the front row. Though I tried to draw him out, he never made eye contact with me.

I make my students write journal entries—five a week—and give them credit just for doing it. I don't mark anything wrong. I usually don't mark anything except points for the completed assignment. However, one day I broke my own rule and marked on this student's journal, because it made me laugh and cry. Next to the red 50/50 I told him how beautiful it was. The next day he smiled.

Soon after that we did an introduction to poetry, in which I asked the students to bring their favorite songs to share with the class. One man brought in a song about saying good-bye to someone you love, and another student shared lyrics about overcoming obstacles to reach your dreams. Another student played her guitar and sang "Eleanor Rigby," and we talked about isolation and how people everywhere need to feel loved. We ended up bonding through the experience of sharing music.

On the last day my quiet student brought his selection.

"I picked this song because it's about this girl who thinks she's ugly, because that's what everyone tells her when she's a kid. But then someone comes along later in her life and tells her she's beautiful, and she starts to believe it and it changes her life," he said.

He proceeded to play "God Loves Ugly" by Jordin Sparks, which says in part: "God loves ugly; He doesn't see the way I see. Oh, God takes ugly and turns it into something that is beautiful. Apparently I'm beautiful, 'cause You love me."

I suppose I've got a reputation for not being conventional in my teaching methods, but I didn't plan to start sobbing hysterically. I just let loose, then and there, in front of the whole class. The student smiled, proud of himself. A few laughed at their nutty professor...and several more cried right along with me.

This wasn't a "Christian" class or a Christian school. It was just a group of people longing for meaning and beauty in a world that often doesn't make sense. Meaning and beauty suddenly showed up in the form of God's love—and it transcended everything.

Suggestion: look for His love and beauty in unexpected places today.

Fishing for Fun

"For you always have the poor with you; but you do not always have Me." MATTHEW 26:11 NASB

I am afflicted with the parasite of productivity, which eats away at my peace. I don't know where I got it; maybe it's my personality. But I tend to believe that if I'm not doing something productive, I'm wasting time. For several years now my kids have been trying to teach me that this is a lie.

I was working at the computer yesterday when my son, Harper, sidled up. Well beyond the description of "avid fisherman" at age six, he started telling me about some bait he wanted to try out. (He studies fishing magazines and saves his allowance of $2.50 per week until he can buy certain lures.) After a discussion of the merits of his new bait, a question or two about what I was working on, and the observation that Dad wasn't home to take him to the pond, it soon became apparent that he wanted to go fishing.

At this point I had a choice. I could have—and a large part of me certainly felt I *should* have—told Harper to go play and leave me alone. After all, we have to pay bills...and although not essential, it's nice to have a little money for the occasional new fishing lure. This is a logic my children are capable of understanding. But there was another bit of logic I felt the Lord reminding me of in that moment. Just the week prior, I'd lamented the start of school and the fact that my big kids weren't home anymore. Now here it was the weekend, and Harper was presenting me with an opportunity to spend time with him while watching him fish.

I looked at Grace and Adelaide, who were both occupied with mindless electronic activity. There was a pile of dishes in the sink and a basket of laundry waiting to be folded. My computer screen blinked back at me with a half-empty page. I thought about how little time I had to get everything done, and then I thought, *I cannot go fishing!*

But, turning back to my children, I began to see time like the expensive oil the woman poured out on Jesus' feet. The disciples thought it was a waste, but they were wrong. Was it really such a waste to go fishing? It was as if Jesus was saying to me, "Your work you have with you always. But your kids are growing up...."

Needless to say, we all piled into the truck and went fishing. It was some of the best time I've ever "wasted"—and the work still got done!

How do you want to remember this day? Look back and see that you said "yes" to what matters and let the rest go.

Days of Mercy

The Dumb-sel in Distress

"When you pass through the waters, I will be with you; and through the rivers, they will not overflow you: when you walk through the fire, you will not be scorched.... For I am the LORD your God...you are precious in My sight...you are honored and I love you...." ISAIAH 43:2–4 NASB

I did a really dumb thing when I was in college. It was the beginning of Christmas break, and I frolicked to a fraternity ball with my friend Zack. Afterward we discovered that my dorm was locked with no way to get in. Zack's solution was to take me with him to the fraternity house where he lived. He was a nice guy whom I trusted, so I decided to go. I didn't see any other viable option.

It was about one in the morning, and there were a few people milling around the house. I went up to Zack's room with him, and he gave me some shorts and a T-shirt so I wouldn't have to sleep in my formal gown.

Like a true gentleman, he lay down on the floor and gave me his bed. I had just dozed off when there came a loud banging on the door. Zack jumped up off the floor to answer it.

My friend Tony charged into the room. "What do you think you're doing?" he demanded. A bewildered Zack tried to explain, but Tony didn't want to hear it.

"Get up!" He motioned to me, gathering my things. "You cannot stay here."

Poor Zack didn't know what to do. "I'm sorry," he said to both of us, as Tony ushered me out of the room. Slamming the door behind us, he whisked me down to his car.

Tony drove across town to his apartment, muttering that it was unacceptable for me to spend the night in a fraternity house under any circumstances.

Bewildered, I said, "I don't understand, Tony. What else could we do?"

"You're not the kind of girl who does that," he stated.

It wasn't Zack's fault, but as Tony talked, I began to see the magnitude of our folly. One of the people in the fraternity who knew us both had seen me and called him. "I couldn't let you ruin your reputation," he explained.

Tony deposited me in his apartment, locked the door behind him, and went to spend the night at the fraternity house himself.

I was saved from a bad situation because—and only because—of the fierce love of a friend. At the fraternity house, I was completely vulnerable without even realizing it.

It's such a beautiful picture of God's mercy. We get ourselves into messes—many times because of our own stupidity—but because of His great mercy we are not consumed. He may not swoop in to save us every time; sometimes we come through the fire a little smoky. But He is there, in His fierce devotion, to set our feet back on solid ground.

In what ways has the Lord demonstrated His mercy toward you lately?

Mercy Comes Through

> "With everlasting kindness I will have mercy
> on you," says the LORD, your Redeemer.

ISAIAH 54:8 NKJV

Mercy was put into perspective for me one time by a friend of mine whose daughter was in great difficulties. This daughter, a Christian, was clinically depressed, had a total lack of energy, was unable to sleep, suffered from migraines, and was gaining weight at an alarming rate. She and her parents had been to all kinds of doctors and tried all kinds of things, but nothing seemed to be helping. After one particularly discouraging day, her mother told me they sat on the floor together just crying out to God.

"We had no words left to pray," she said. "All we could say over and over was, 'Lord Jesus, Son of God, have mercy on us!' "

All throughout the Gospels we see people saying that to Jesus. Blind men, lepers, people possessed with demons, parents begging for their children to be healed... And every single time Jesus responds to them with compassion. He sees their needs and reaches out to meet them on the deepest level.

My friend's daughter finally got her hormone issues straightened out and, with medication, now lives a life free of depression. But going to that place of complete devastation—actually throwing themselves at the mercy of God—showed her and her parents something that helps keep them in right relationship with God. They were forced to recognize their utter dependence on Him. After exploring everything man had to offer, they were completely out of options when mercy came through. He kept them going and eventually led her out of the darkness.

That story is actually just a snapshot of reality—a reality I'm often too slow to acknowledge. I go about my days fairly independently, weighing my options on how to raise my children, what to do for work, how to manage finances, and how to best meet my own needs and the needs of others. Sometimes I lose sight of the fact that I don't have supernatural resources to do any of this. In a spiritual sense, I am completely dependent on the mercy of God.

The good news is that He freely gives us all the mercy we need, and it never runs out. There is mercy for little things like mopping the floor. Mercy for doing the laundry. There's mercy for dealing with that person—again—or mercy for walking away. There's mercy for things we don't understand, mercy for our heartaches, mercy for our failures. Mercy for our triumphs and joys.

"Oh, give thanks to the Lord, for He is good! For His mercy endures forever" (1 Chronicles 16:34 NKJV).

Jesus, Son of God, I need Your mercy for... (fill in the blank).

Rags to Riches

*But as for me, I will enter Your house through
the abundance of Your steadfast love and mercy;
I will worship...in reverent fear and awe of You.*

PSALM 5:7 AMP

I love today's verse. I love it because I often come to
the Lord empty. Empty-handed, wearing filthy rags, and
empty down in my soul, with a painful longing to be
satisfied and yet the shameful knowledge that I have
absolutely nothing to offer in the exchange. No talent,
no beauty or intelligence, no material thing, no gift
that would enhance His existence at all. There's not a
single solitary reason He would want to let me enter
His house. And yet the Bible says I can enter through
the abundance of His steadfast love and mercy.

I picture myself, this grubby pauper lifting a stained
hand to knock on the door. But even before I can make
a sound, the door is thrown open wide and my Father
steps forward to greet me. Jesus is there, in all of His

shining radiance, and all I can do is fall on my face and worship. My rags are exchanged for the riches of His kingdom. My fears are infused with His courage. My weakness gives way to His power, and my shame is swallowed up by His love. He brushes the dirt off my face, wraps me in His royal robe, and calls me His daughter. I'm home!

This relationship is a great mystery—how we can be loved with the familiarity of a family, totally secure in knowing that He is always with us—and yet God as a being is so very different from us. His ways are past finding out. He is high and lifted up. He is totally different—beyond our comprehension. Bono, lead singer of U2, said: "The idea that there's a force of love and logic behind the universe is overwhelming to start with...but the idea that that same love and logic would choose to describe itself as a baby born in...straw and poverty is genius and brings me to my knees, literally.... I am just in awe of that.... It's the thing that makes me a believer."

There's a terror to worshiping God, to contemplating His holiness. But that reverent fear, like a flower reaching out to the sun, finds its nourishment—its fulfillment—in the abundance of His love. He is the great and mighty King, but He invites us to enter. To come as we are.

When I come before the Lord, one thing He gives me in exchange for my emptiness is awe...an awe that someone like Him would come to earth in order to save someone like me. What a mystery. What a Savior!

What riches of the kingdom will you tap in order to make this a beautiful day?

Broken Beauty

To all who mourn...he will give: beauty for ashes; joy
instead of mourning; praise instead of heaviness.
For God has planted them like strong and graceful
oaks for his own glory. Isaiah 61:3 TLB

I met Lauren the day she shuffled into my class. I say *shuffled* because although she had the face and body of a Barbie doll, she moved like a very old woman. This irony puzzled me, so, being the nosy teacher that I am, I asked her to tell me her story.

Lauren's parents divorced when she was little. She had one sister, and they were very close. In high school both girls were popular. They won beauty contests and had lots of friends, but they started drinking and going to parties. By the time they were in college, they were doing drugs. Lauren was living with her boyfriend when she found out she was pregnant. Her sister was pregnant, too.

Lauren told me, "I immediately stopped drinking and

stuff, but my sister couldn't quit. She was afraid she was damaging her baby, so she got an abortion. That was when she really changed."

Her sister descended into deep depression. When Lauren gave birth to a healthy baby boy, her sister celebrated with her. But he also reminded her of the decision she herself had made, and it ate away at her soul.

"I got a call one night that my sister was dead," Lauren said. "She left a suicide note that said she was sorry and how much she loved me and my baby, but she just couldn't take the pain anymore. I was completely devastated."

Reeling from this loss, Lauren herself emotionally plunged over the edge. "My son was the only reason I didn't kill myself," she confessed, "but I did everything I could to escape reality."

One night when her child was with her mother, Lauren got high on drugs in her second-story apartment. Hearing someone at the door and fearful of being caught, she jumped out of the window.

"I hit the ground and heard my bones crack and

crunch. I lay there thinking, 'I'm going to die.' "

When Lauren was taken to the emergency room, she heard voices of people beside her bed: "She probably won't make it." "If she does, she'll never walk."

"I laid there for five hours," Lauren said. "I could feel my spirit slipping from my body, and I begged God, *Please don't let it end this way. Please let me be a mother to my son.*"

God saw her where she was, and He heard her prayer.

"He saved my life, but more than that, He saved my soul. And now He's even letting me walk again!"

Lauren lives with the scars and enduring pain of her bad choices. But when you get to know her, all you see is beauty. Strength. Grace.

"Jesus is real!" She bubbles over with joy. "And with Him, nothing is impossible—I am living proof of that. No matter what I've lost, I feel like I've gained everything, just because I know Him now. He is with me—no matter what."

Ask God to help you pick up the broken pieces in your life and put them together. He can create a mosaic that will be beautiful!

"Mucher"

May God give you more and more mercy,
peace, and love. JUDE 1:2 NLT

My little niece Sophia says the funniest things.

This past summer, she and her family took a trip to Gulf Shores, Alabama. Sophia enjoyed chasing after sand crabs with a net. When she caught one, however, she didn't want to touch it for fear it would "sharp" her. One evening when they were cooking tacos, she told her mother she would help her find "taco shells" on the beach. And on the day they were packing to leave, she informed her sister, Madeline, that unfortunately Madeline would have to stay in Gulf Shores while the rest of the family went home.

Sophia's partner-in-crime is my daughter Adelaide. Because Sophia is ten months older, she gets to boss Adelaide sometimes, at least in theory. Sophia master-minded two games they play all the time called "Honey" and "Ma'am." I believe the way "Honey" is played is that they call one another "honey" as they carry their dolls around, basically playing house. "Ma'am" works much the same way but is played in a shopping setting.

Presumably because Adelaide's name is hard to pronounce, Sophia very early on gave her the nickname "Ass," to the chagrin of her mother. "Ass" and I love having Sophia over to play, and I always buy her favorite foods when she is coming. The other day Sophia was at our house for a visit. Because she loves strawberries and cantaloupe, we had both in abundance and brought them out at snack time. "Ooh, straw-beddies!" Adelaide squealed. I gave them both a heaping bowlful.

When Sophia had stuffed her mouth full of strawberries, she held out her bowl. "I want some mucher," she told me, so I gave her another spoonful. "Mucher!" she said, and I heaped on more. With her aquamarine eyes dancing, she giggled. "Mucher and mucher and mucher!" This went on till her bowl was again full. I knew she couldn't possibly eat them all, but I wanted her to have as many as she could hold.

A little while later I curled up in the middle of Sophia and Adelaide for a nap, and while they slept, I thought about the concept of "mucher." It's a cute way of saying *more*, of course, as illustrated by the strawberries. But what I want most for my girls, and what I myself need, is not more strawberries. It's more and more of Jesus. Mucher and mucher and mucher. And because of His mercy, He freely gives us all our hearts can hold.

May your day be filled with the beauty of Jesus—mucher of His goodness, mucher of His power, mucher of His love!

Days of Joy

A Good Boy

The Lord thy God in the midst of thee is mighty; he
will save, he will rejoice over thee with joy; he will
rest in his love, he will joy over thee with singing.

Zephaniah 3:17 kjv

My sister-in-law Rene told me a funny story about
my brother Jim the other day. She was telling him how
it can be hard for her to accept that God loves her, even
though she knows it's true.

"Do you ever have that problem?" she had asked Jim.
"I mean, do you ever think He knows the things you're
capable of and just can't get past it? That He can love
other people but He could never love you?"

My brother looked at her and laughed. "No, I don't.
I mean, I know I'm a sinner just like everyone else, but
I honestly don't ever think that way. I believe God is
actually quite fond of me."

Rene chuckled then. "What do you mean?"

"Well, just the other day I was sitting at my desk,

sort of praying and just thinking about my day, all the things I had to do, and how I wanted to make good decisions in my job. It's not always easy. But in that moment I felt God speaking to my heart. He said, '*Jim, you're a good boy.*' "

Rene and I had a good laugh over that, since both of us, who love him so much, also know how ornery he can be. But I thought about that story again this morning when my son came in the house, to where I was reading in bed. It was still early, but already he'd been outside with Stone, dealing with a tree that had fallen over, and he brought in some damp mistletoe.

"Mom, look what I found."

He held it over my head, dripping, and gave me a kiss.

"Good morning, Harper. Did you have a good night's sleep?"

"Mom, I thought of happy stuff just like you told me to, and I didn't have any bad dreams. I had this dream about fishing, though, and I caught a huge catfish, the hugest you've ever seen, and it bent my pole and I could barely get it in but I did...."

His eyes were shining. His hair was sticking up. He

still had on his pajamas. And in that moment I was reminded: there is nothing I would rather do in life than be his mother, the one he tells his fishing stories to, the one who tucks him in at night.

Harper was born a sinner, and sometimes he makes mistakes. He's ornery like his uncle. But he's a good boy. And I'm quite fond of him, just as I believe the Father is fond of us.

God not only loves you, but He likes you, too. In fact, He's crazy about you. You're a child of the King, and He thinks you're a good one!

A New Thing

"Forget the former things; do not dwell on the past.
See, I am doing a new thing!" ISAIAH 43:18–19 NIV

My parents are building a new house, which is cause for great joy and celebration...and a little bit of trauma. Building a new house means they soon will be leaving their old one behind. And our family has a lot of sentimental ties to that old one.

My grandparents moved to Ozark when my mother was a little girl. Their small farm on the hill was a refuge for them as they fled the big city. When my mother married my father, my grandparents gave them land on the hill to build their dream house, which they did. That house is where my brother and I were raised.

All of our memories are associated with that place on the hill. But for some time now it seems the Lord has been doing something new.

With my brother and me finally off the payroll—out of college and established—my parents were able to buy a ranch south of Ozark that overlooks the Arkansas River. Following in the tradition of my grandparents, they gave both of us our picks of the land for a place to build our own dreams. We've been living out here for several years now, enjoying the view and the farm and especially the fellowship. Our kids run back and forth between our houses, sharing every childhood joy we hoped they would.

The only thing missing has been my parents. Now, it's not all that bad by most standards; they live only fifteen minutes away. But for people like us who are into communal-like living, it's kind of a long ways. At the end of every get-together, when my brother's family and mine can wave good-bye down the path between our houses, they have to get in the car and go home. When Dad wants to work in his garden or take care of his cows, he has to come across the river. And when Mom wants to see her grandkids, they're not right across the field like my brother and I were with Granny on the hill.

Since my parents finally decided to build a new house on the ranch, the process has been a new journey of faith. We've seen how painful it is to let go of the past and move on into something new, even when that new thing is exciting. It's hard. But in the end, if we trust the Lord, new things can lead us to the new heights of joy that He has planned, like watching the first snowfall over the river with your mother or seeing your grand-baby coming down the path to your door.

What new thing is the Lord doing in your life? Embrace it today!

Water Baby

God has given us these times of joy.

PSALM 81:4 TLB

Rene and I took our kids to a water park the other day, setting up headquarters in the baby pool area, where the youngest kids would play. Rene stayed there with them, while I was assigned to the bigger kids, consisting of my oldest two, Grace and Harper, and my niece Madeline.

Grace and Harper headed straight for the waterslides. They went up the stairs, stood in the lines, and slid down several times while Madeline patiently looked on. I mostly stayed at the bottom with her, watching.

"Do you want to slide, sweetie?"

"Nope." It was too scary; she wasn't going to budge.

After several minutes, I decided it was time for us to move on. Grace and Harper showed no signs of waning in their sliding zeal, and they seemed fine to navigate the park without me as long as they stayed together. It was Madeline's turn to pick something to do.

She led me to a section where we could run through rainbow-shaped sprinklers. Next we shot each other with water that spouted from purple elephants' trunks. After that we went to a pool that was three feet deep, and she slid down a miniature slide into my arms. Then she wanted to swim in the "big pool," which was four feet deep and over her head.

Snapping on her Barbie life jacket, we got in and she paddled around. After she got comfortable, she wanted to jump off the side. I stayed in the pool to catch her, having been given strict instructions not to let her go under the water.

As I stood there waiting, the magic of the moment overwhelmed me and I had to hold back my tears. She perched on the edge of the pool, waving me forward and back till she judged the perfect distance, and then she held up her hand as if to say "Stop." Our eyes locked and then she bent her little bird legs and leaped, with wild abandon, into my arms. The sound of her laughter rang in my ears.

"Give me a boost," she urged me, and I thrusted her toward the ladder, where she climbed up to do it again.

Over and over she jumped to me, throwing her arms around my neck, and with each time it got harder for me to let her go. See, she starts kindergarten this year. And just like Grace and Harper, who used to jump to me, next year she'll probably be ready for the slides. These days we have together—such beautiful days of joy—are laced with the awareness that life is fleeting.

O Lord, let me savor every moment. Give me the wisdom to live and love with my whole heart.

Let It Be

Godliness with contentment is great gain.

1 TIMOTHY 6:6 KJV

If I am honest, I have to admit that I have trouble with contentment and resting in the Lord. At least in my mind. It's constantly busy—active, imagining, analyzing something. I'm not thinking only about important things, but I'm never thinking about nothing.

I've always been this way to a certain extent, but more so since I became a mother. When you're responsible for small children, there's a sense that you should always be doing something. That might be because there's always something that needs to be done. And it's hard to be content with those things hanging over your head.

Take last night, for instance. I had plans, after dinner and dishes, to go walking before it was time for baths and bed. When those plans were thwarted by a storm, the family saw a great opportunity to settle in playing games or watching a movie. I saw an opportunity to do laundry, write thank-you notes, and put pictures in an album. After all, those things needed to be done.

While Stone and the oldest two wrestled on the floor, our two-year-old dug through a drawer of movies. She shocked us all by exclaiming in rapturous delight, "We have *Barney!*"

Apparently she has seen Barney on TV at her cousins' house. I guess she never knew we had Barney movies. She was so adorable when she asked me to watch one with her that I couldn't resist. I left the laundry piled on the couch and sat down with her in our big brown chair.

As my daughter watched Barney sing and dance, I realized how easy it is for a child to just "be." She leaned back, drinking her bottle of milk, and soaked it in. There seemed to be nothing else on her mind, no sense of what she should be doing; she was just content. I envied her a little, but I also felt convicted.

When is it we learn that we always need to be doing something? Someone has said we don't have to—otherwise we'd be called human *doings* instead of human *beings*. But sometimes it's so much easier to *do* than to just *be*.

I have a theory about this. Constantly doing seems to validate our existence. It makes us feel more important. Like on *Survivor*, we're trying to prove our worth to the tribe...and perhaps to ourselves.

However, God says to be content. He calls us not to be lazy and never get anything done, but to balance our work with rest. And even when we're at work, to rest our souls in Him. Not to be always thinking, analyzing, and planning, but to stay our minds on Him and live in peace.

Even though the whole world seems busy, busy, busy...choose contentment. Do only the work He appoints, and then let the rest be.

The Small-Town Sisterhood

If we walk in the light as He is in the light, we have fellowship with one another. 1 John 1:7 NKJV

A few years ago, some friends and I were feeling the lack of feminine connection in our lives. Most of us were married with kids, jobs, and plenty of social obligations, but we weren't spending much time nurturing friendships with other women, especially those outside of our intimate circles. Some of us had been in sororities that kept records of attendance and required community service, but that felt too structured. We decided to create a sisterhood that would meet once a month just for the purpose of having fun.

These girls are from different backgrounds. We go to different churches, do different things, live different lives. But once a month we come together at somebody's house, eat a meal, and talk. Sometimes we plan other activities, but we don't always get around to them. Mostly we talk. About our families and lives, ideas that interest us, and issues that concern us. It's a glorious thing.

I don't know when it occurred to me that this is fellowship. It's something we're made for and called to do. From the new mother to the grandmother, the doctor to the housewife, the Catholic to the Baptist— we all have something we personally need and something we can offer each other.

I am especially blessed by this group. As a writer and stay-at-home mom who only teaches classes a couple of days a week, I can tend toward hermit-ness. I live out in the country, and a lot of my life goes on within a half-mile radius. But it's great to get out once a month and listen to the lives of other women. They require my attention and willingness to give of myself, but they also support me, enrich me, and help to keep me balanced. Our gatherings always remind me that community is important. No man or woman is an island. The plan was never for us to go it alone.

This was the way of the early church. They met in each other's homes, broke bread, and shared their lives with one another—the good and the bad. But in our time, we seem to lose out on fellowship unless we are intentional about it. The Sisterhood sets one night aside each month and puts it on the calendar. We don't keep attendance, but everybody tries to make it as much as they can. And for some it's become essential—a tool for survival in a busy world.

Sometimes when we're all together I get the sense that God is pleased, that He's there among His daughters. He's all about investing in relationships. I think He delights in seeing us connect and hearing us laugh. And I believe our joy is beautiful to Him.

How are you making time for community in your life? It's time to get intentional about this beautiful gift of God.

Snorkeling in Jesus

Your eyes will see the King in his beauty....
The glorious Lord will be to us as a wide river.
ISAIAH 33:17, 21 TLB

Donald Miller, in his brilliant book *Blue Like Jazz*, mentions hearing a Native American speaker say that God was in the water. Don writes that he thought "how beautiful that was because it meant you could swim in Him." I thought about that idea this summer, as I watched my eight-year-old trying to snorkel in the ocean off the coast of Florida's panhandle.

With her seven-dollar mask and a hand-me-down snorkel, Grace played in the waves at the water's edge. She asked me to go in with her a little farther, so we walked out to where the water came just above my knees. "Hold on to me," she commanded. I stood nearby, always touching her while she looked underwater for shells and signs of docile marine life. Once she came up for a breath with seaweed in her hair. After struggling in vain a good while to find something exciting, Grace tossed her snorkel and mask up on the beach. "I don't see what the big deal is about snorkeling. I can't see anything but sand."

Now, I've had the privilege of snorkeling on one of the premier coral reefs of the world—near a village called Da'hab on the Red Sea. There are no words to describe the beauty I beheld there. As my back was being burned to a crisp on top of the water, my eyes were drawn into a whole new Technicolor world—a fantasy of wild colors and shapes, a dance choreographed to celestial music.

I'm not knocking the Gulf of Mexico or the lovely American beaches that border it. The seafood is great, and I love the sugary-white sand of the places we haunt on our family vacations. But no snorkeling experience so far has ever come close to the Red Sea. Maybe nothing else will.

Understanding Grace's frustration, I told her about Da'hab. Her eyes widened with wonder, and she asked if we could go there sometime.

Later, as I thought about Grace and her desire to see something special, I thought about Jesus and how beautiful He is. Sometimes we get stuck in the murky water of religion and we think that's all there is—rules and regulations, rituals we've kept so long we don't even know why we do it anymore. Religion drowns our joy. But there's a whole other world out there, as different from religion as a coral reef is from seaweed and sand.

I want to live in that world and share it with others. And while I hope Grace can snorkel Da'hab someday, more than that I want her to see Jesus and know Him—in all of His splendor.

Suggestion for the day: go swimming in the sea of God's grace. His wonders never cease!

Days of Peace

85 Percent

It is better to trust and take refuge in the Lord
than to put confidence in man. Psalm 118:8 amp

One of my friends has a son named Von who was diagnosed with leukemia at age three. Von is now four, and the rigorous treatment he's been undergoing seems to be working. Our family has joined with his in praying and believing that Von will be totally restored to good health.

Throughout this journey, my friend has kept a blog that we've followed in order to keep up with Von and the family's prayer needs. It's amazing to me the amount of grace that rests on my friend as he walks through this time with his only son. I read the blog in order to know how to pray and be a blessing to the family, but more often than not I come away with spiritual insight that blesses me.

One of my favorite entries shows my friend's perspective on peace and where to truly find it. I asked him if I could include it in this book because it speaks so profoundly to the issue of what constitutes a beautiful day. The entry reads as follows:

> Today was a really good day. I enjoyed the gift of the day, the people around me, the food before me, and the sunshine outside. It's amazing how good the things of today become when you are unsure of the things of tomorrow. And it's funny how our finite human minds want assurances for those days ahead.
>
> Von's life expectancy is one of those areas where we want an assurance. The doctors are squeamish about throwing out numbers, which I respect. If you press them, they won't tell you that Von has an 85 percent chance of living or a 15 percent chance of dying; they will tell you that the incidents of his type of cancer see an 85 percent cure rate.
>
> Cure rate/chance of living...call it what you want; the temptation for me this week has been to look to a percentage and cling to it for some sense of comfort and put my heart at ease. And in that number, I have found no hope or sense of comfort.

I've asked myself if a 90 percent would make me feel a lot better or a little better. What about 95 percent? I raised it to a 100 percent chance of living, and even that felt empty.

Through this, I was reminded that God is the only thing I can look to or find comfort in. He knows the number of my days. He knows the number of Von's days. I have given Von's future over to Him, and in that I find a sense of peace that God has a plan and it will all work out in the right way and time.

Yep, today was a good day.

Is there something you're trying to answer through the wisdom of man? Look to God instead. His heart for you is hope and peace.

The Saga of the Goat

When you turn to the right or when you turn to the left, your ears shall hear a word behind you, saying, "This is the way; walk in it." Isaiah 30:21 NRSV

We have this goat named Vincent Van Goat. He's an Egyptian pygmy, but on the inside he's huge. His attitude is such that he has earned the nickname "Gruff," as in the three billy goats.

Our kids love Vincent. They take cookies out to his pen and let him eat from their hands. His pen has plenty of playing room, clean water, food, and even a little stable with hay where he can sleep at night. The stable is made of tin and cedar, and the kids and I painted it, giving it flair.

You'd think, for such a little goat, Vincent's pen would be great. It's in the shade, with trees all around when he wants to nibble on a leaf. My husband put in a big stump that Vincent likes to get up on and play king of the mountain. We keep everything nice and clean.

But every chance that goat sees, he gets out of his pen. I'm not really sure how he does it.

The first time he escaped, we came home to find him in the yard. He was lying under a tree munching some grass and looked up lazily at us. Seduced by a treat, he followed my husband back into his pen. Stone thought he could see where the goat had gotten out, so he tightened the fence in that area. But the next day, Vincent escaped again.

This went on for several days. Every time Vincent got out, we'd inspect the pen and make adjustments until there were no more places to tighten. We thought the pen was Houdini-proof. When we went on vacation, we asked my brother's family next door to tend to Vincent for us. The day we left, my brother found the goat on his front porch, eating flowers.

Vincent's antics have me thinking about God's peace. See, the reason we keep Vincent in a pen is for his safety, especially at night. We live out in the wild wilderness, and the occasional mountain lion and coyotes abound. Vincent, with his miniature size, wouldn't stand a chance against them.

God's peace, for me, is like Vincent's pen. It's a great place, designed for my safety, where my heart can rest. When I stay within those boundaries, no matter what is ready to devour me, I know I'm okay. But when I act outside of His peace, going my own way in spite of the still, small voice saying "This way!" I'm making a mistake. And the consequences are often more serious than a few nibbled flowers.

Lord, I'm sorry for fighting You when You're only trying to protect me. Today I choose the safety of Your peace.

Comparison,
the Silent Killer

*Thou wilt keep him in perfect peace, whose mind
is stayed on thee: because he trusteth in thee.*

ISAIAH 26:3 KJV

There's a disease running rampant today, stealing our joy, our peace, and even our purpose. It sucks the beauty out of our days. It's wrong to infect ourselves and spread it to others, yet we all carry it to some degree. It's called *comparison*.

It looks like this: a woman walks into a room looking drop-dead gorgeous. She's wearing the latest fashion; her body is toned, her hair perfectly coiffed, her nails professionally done, and her makeup flawless. Unless we guard ourselves against comparison, every other woman in the room shrinks just a little. We look down at our unpainted nails or run our fingers through our mousy hair. We suck in our stomachs or fidget with the tassel on last year's sweater, and somewhere inside us a voice whispers, *You're not good enough. You'll never be like her.*

Simultaneously, as we're internalizing this comparison, we're also projecting it onto a creature God made and loves. We're assessing her value by her outward appearance, not even giving her heart a chance. And if today we're a little bit jealous, next time we may be relieved to see that she's gained weight or her roots are showing. A new comparison may take her down a notch or two—and build us back up.

But this isn't just about outward appearance, no. It can be about anything. Consider this ridiculous personal scenario: A writer experiences moderate success with her first couple of books. She goes to a conference and meets other writers who are also successful, some more so than she. She realizes how big the world of publishing is versus how small her experience. She comes home deflated, wondering if she has what it takes. Instead of getting her answer from the Lord, she surfs the Internet, reading book reviews, blogs, and Web pages of other writers. She becomes convinced that she will never be like them—never good enough—so she doesn't write anything else. (At least for a while, anyway.)

What is the cure for this common malady? Like today's verse says, we have to keep our minds on Him. If I'm thinking about Jesus, trusting Him with my life, family, looks, health, intellect, work, etc., He has promised to keep me in perfect peace. He's our "vaccination," if you will, against all the complications caused by the comparison virus.

I'd like to start a revolution called *No Comparison*. Let's be kinder to ourselves and others. Let's refuse to judge another person based on his or her appearance or performance. And when the temptation comes to compare ourselves, whether for better or worse, let's resist it in the power of peace. Let's keep our minds where they belong: on Him.

No Comparison, all day. That goes for me and for others. I'm keeping my mind on Jesus.

His Approval

I'm not trying to win the approval of people, but of God. If pleasing people were my goal, I would not be Christ's servant. GALATIANS 1:10 NLT

I heard a quote once that has stayed with me. It's from Don Lessin, lifetime missionary to Mexico and older brother to my friend Roy. Don said this: *I'd like to have your approval, but I can live without it. I cannot live without God's.*

Apparently Don said this after he made a controversial decision. He'd pastored a church in one place in Mexico for several years, and the Lord blessed his ministry. But when Don felt the Lord calling him to move to a different city, many people did not want him to leave. Don said he tried to explain as best he could, but in the end it boiled down to this: no matter who disagreed with him, he had to follow the Lord's direction for his path.

For someone like me who likes to please other people, Don's quote is a great simplifier of life. Not only do I hate disappointing non-Christian friends and colleagues, I really, really hate to face disapproval from my Christian brothers and sisters. It seems that if we're all hearing from God, then we should all be on the same page. But that's certainly not true in my experience, and it's actually not even biblical.

Consider the story in Acts 13 of how Paul, Barnabas, and John Mark go out together witnessing. They have all these great spiritual experiences and no problem is ever mentioned...but then there's a little verse tucked away between scenes that says: "Now Paul and his companions sailed from Paphos and came to Perga in Pamphylia. And John [Mark] separated himself from them and went back to Jerusalem" (v. 13 AMP).

Later, in chapter 15, Barnabas wants to bring John Mark back on board with them, but Paul doesn't—so they split up. Barnabas and John Mark went to Cyprus, and Paul and Silas took off for Syria (Acts 15:37–41 AMP).

Why is this significant? These were all godly men. And it illustrates the fact that God speaks different things to different people. Though I don't believe He contradicts Himself, I do believe He takes into account our unique gifts. He gave them to us. And that means you may not worship the same way I do or share the same convictions about what to drink or how to dress. Church may not look the same for us and we may not agree on every doctrine. But I can respect and learn from you and give you room to grow, just as I hope you will do for me.

And if the Lord directs your path in a direction I don't understand or agree with, I hope I'll still support you. If I don't, remember that you can live without my approval—but you cannot live without His.

Lord, help me listen for Your voice above all others and look to You alone for approval.

Hope vs. Optimism

Hope does not disappoint us, because God has poured out his love into our hearts by the Holy Spirit, whom he has given us. ROMANS 5:5 NIV

I was listening to NPR this morning on the way home after I dropped my kids off at school. There was an interview with a famous author from Uruguay whose book Hugo Chavez recently gave as a gift to our American president. It seemed the book was at least in part about the exploitation and pillaging of South American resources by capitalist countries like our own.

I don't understand the politics of it all, but what I could relate to was the author's frustration with the imperfection of the world, especially as manifested through greed. He talked a lot about the poor and how he would like to see the great gulf reduced between the rich and the poor people of the world.

At one point the journalist asked him something like, "The themes of your work are very dark. Are you a person of optimism? Or do you see no hope for our current situation?"

Paraphrased, the author's answer was, "Some days I wake up with hope, but then I plunge down to the floor by midday. I may find something to lift me up that afternoon, but then the darkness usually overwhelms me. I find it hard to stay optimistic."

The thing that struck me about this conversation was the interchangeable uses of *hope* and *optimism*. It's similar to how some people confuse the words *happiness* and *joy*. On the surface they may seem the same, but as a Christian, I've come to see that hope is not the same thing as optimism any more than happiness is joy.

Optimism is based on feeling. We may wake up with it and then something bad may happen to make it go away. Because it's associated with feelings, it's impossible to constantly maintain—because we can't always control what we feel. Most of the time our feelings are reactions to our circumstances.

Hope is different. Like joy, it is based on something much deeper than our feelings; it's based on the sovereign goodness of God. I may be just as distressed as this guy from Uruguay about the world's problems, but my hope is not built on the election of a president or the fulfillment of any human ideal. It's built on the promise that God is in control.

If I really believe this, it's not some shallow claim that absolves me of social responsibility. On the contrary, hope motivates me to participate in bringing about the kingdom of God on earth. In Jesus I have something much better than optimism to offer the poor and downtrodden. Hope—and the spreading of it—is the bedrock of our faith.

Lord, how can I be a hope-spreader today?

What Forgiveness Isn't

If it is possible, as far as it depends on you,
live at peace with everyone. ROMANS 12:18 NIV

One of the biggest struggles I've had as a Christian was with forgiveness. My greatest struggle has been more with the *nature* of forgiveness—what forgiveness actually *is*—rather than the difficulty of forgiving someone in and of itself.

Like many Christians, I've heard plenty of teaching about the importance of forgiveness. I know about "seventy times seven," and I know the Bible says that if we don't forgive others God won't forgive us (Matthew 18:22, Mark 11:26 NASB). I've heard countless speakers say that we must forgive and forget because that's what God does. What seems to follow such advice is that if we can just forgive whoever wronged us, all will be well. The relationship will be restored, and we can live at peace. But what about those times when the other person isn't sorry?

What if he or she apologizes but continues in the behavior? What are we supposed to do then?

This was my agonizing question. For years I tried to have a relationship with a person I desperately loved and wanted to please. I know I'm not perfect, but the best I knew how I gave my heart to this person, trying to share the life of Jesus. My efforts were constantly met with derision. Sometimes I'd spend a day with this person and then be physically ill for two weeks. Those encounters were the most stressful times of my life.

Looking back, I wonder what psychosis kept me in that relationship for so long. At least part of my reasoning was a sense of duty as a Christian, a hope that I could win the person over. I also had a skewed sense of what it means to forgive.

I remember praying, "Lord, I choose to forgive. I choose to love this person." I would move forward from there thinking that I was free from the pain and could somehow go back into the relationship with a clean slate. But the abuse would happen again.

This pattern continued till I finally began to learn what forgiveness *isn't*. And I'm sorry to say it isn't what seems to be the popular Christian mentality. One day I read the story in 1 Samuel of how Saul tried to kill David. A new observation popped out at me: David forgave Saul and still loved him, but David didn't go back to Saul for more. He *fled and escaped* (1 Samuel 19:18 KJV).

Forgiveness of others is essential to peace with God. But just like David, we cannot create peace with a person who continues in behavior that hurts us. Sometimes forgiveness means we love someone who hates us...from a safe distance.

Don't use it as a cop-out, but if you've done all you can do, create some distance and enjoy His peace.

Crazy Days

What I Learned from Michael Jackson

Do you think anyone is going to be able to drive a wedge between us and Christ's love for us? There is no way! Not trouble, not hard times, not hatred, not hunger, not homelessness, not bullying threats, not backstabbing, not even the worst sins listed in Scripture.... None of this fazes us because Jesus loves us. I'm absolutely convinced that nothing—nothing living or dead, angelic or demonic, today or tomorrow, high or low, thinkable or unthinkable—absolutely nothing can get between us and God's love because of the way that Jesus our Master has embraced us.

ROMANS 8:35, 37–39 THE MESSAGE

I went a little crazy when Michael Jackson died. I know that sounds weird, and I don't fully understand it myself. I wasn't a fan as a kid. As an adult I'd practically forgotten he existed. But when the story of his death—

and subsequent analyses of his life—flooded the media, I became intrigued.

My parents could tell you that this was not an isolated occurrence. Through the years I've had fleeting obsessions with othe tragic figures—JFK, RFK, MLK...Marilyn Monroe, Elvis, Princess Di, Heath Ledger.... Their stories all fascinate me.

What captivated me most about Michael Jackson, once I started reading about his life, was his genius. I don't think I ever appreciated it before he died. I lived in the boonies as a kid, and we didn't get MTV. I wasn't that crazy about his music, and some of his dance moves were definitely obscene (while others were amazing). But as I dug into his story, what emerged out of all of it was the sense of a person who was absolutely brilliant at his craft.

As a writer, that's just cool to witness. It's challenging. I think it's something every artist aspires to, but some people are born with it—a gift that surpasses the ordinary, like what the Brontë sisters had for writing and Picasso for painting. Like Michael Jackson had for music and dance.

When I recognized he was one of those people and not just another celebrity whose ambition made a mess of his life, it mattered to me somehow. Gifts like that come from God. And beyond the sad waste of a human life, which is precious, his death also felt like a waste—a squandering—of something else. Something special and spiritual, or something that could have been.

What I learned from Michael Jackson, which I suppose I already knew, is that performing for others doesn't ultimately lead to joy. That's apparently true even if one is supremely gifted. People will be disappointed in us sometimes, and even the best of them will let us down. One simply can't ride the flow of popular opinion and remain standing. We have to have a center that holds or, as the poet Yeats says, *things fall apart*.

That strong center is Jesus. His loving acceptance is all we need, which never wavers. I don't know if he would have listened, but I wish I could have told Michael Jackson that.

Thank You, Lord, that no matter what my performance is, You love and accept me. Help me draw my security always and only from You.

There and Back Again

*Most of all, love each other as if your life depended
on it. Love makes up for practically anything.*

1 PETER 4:8 THE MESSAGE

The book providing the backdrop to J.R.R. Tolkien's
great Lord of the Rings trilogy is called *The Hobbit, or
There and Back Again*. It tells the story of Bilbo Baggins's
perilous adventure from his hobbit hole into a whole
other world. Several times along the journey Bilbo
thinks he will never make it home again, but eventually
he does, later recording his travels in a volume he calls
There and Back Again.

I feel like I've been "there and back again" when it
comes to the issue of homosexuality. My approach for
years has been to try to love everybody since Jesus
does, and since that seems hard enough, I've never gone
much further than that. Having known different gay
people throughout my life but never anyone very close
to me, it's an issue I've been able to conveniently skirt.

I know what the Bible says. I've heard it interpreted by plenty of different sources. But in the last few years, as I've been asked about my view on the subject, I've never felt a peace about my answer.

It seems the Lord has allowed it to become personal. Close friends have struggled with the issue and I've not known how to help. Already searching, I ran into someone I hadn't seen in years—a Christian friend who had been almost like a brother before I got married and we went our separate ways.

This guy told me how he had wrestled with God, finally facing the fact that he was gay. "I begged God to change me so I could get married, have kids, and live a normal life, but He hasn't. This is who I am." He went on to tell me about a Bible study he's in and talked about alternative ways of reading the Scriptures about homosexuality.

My brain hurt with the effort of trying to understand. I'll admit I couldn't. At one point the tears streamed down my face, and I said to my friend, "I don't know what all the answers are or if we'll ever agree on theology. But there is one thing I do know, and that is I love you and I will never stop."

After that I did some research, trying to learn more so that maybe I could help others...but the more I read, the crazier I began to feel. Finally I felt the Spirit turning me back again to a place very close to where I started.

I don't usually know what God is up to. I must trust His work in the lives of others, believing He'll get them where He wants them to go. And even though I don't have all the answers, I do have love. And love is enough, as Peter says, for practically everything.

Who might need to see the unconditional love of Jesus reaching out through you today?

Breaking the Bread

> *"I am the bread of life; he who comes
> to Me will not hunger, and he who believes
> in Me will never thirst."* JOHN 6:35 NASB

One time on a trip to San Francisco, I was treated to a meal at the Zuni Café. The chef there is world-famous, and so is the brick oven that forms the centerpiece of the café. The architecture is clean and simple, with wood and windows everywhere, so it is filled with natural light. You feel sort of California-chic just being there, except when you have to order and then remember that you're really a Southern hick.

I had a very patient server who explained to me all the words on the menu I didn't know, which were embarrassingly numerous and ranged from sauces to types of cheese to brands of wine. I don't think he'd ever met anyone from Arkansas. I'd never ordered a twenty-five-dollar hamburger.

One of the fun things about eating at Zuni is that they

bring you this incredible bread. The bread is good...and it comes with a chunk of butter that looks like it's been hacked off a block just made in the kitchen.

The person I was with doesn't eat wheat, so it was up to me to consume the bread, which I did with gusto. Perhaps recognizing my fervor, the waiter offered to bring some more with our meal. I asked for a box for the leftover, imagining myself with the bread and some artisan cheese in the hotel—snack heaven.

Zuni Café is on a major thoroughfare, and if you walk from there toward Union Square, you'll pass people playing chess in front of the United Nations building. Right in front of the chess people, I was approached by a homeless man.

"Spare a bite of food for someone who's starving?"

"Sure," I said, handing him the stylish brown box.

I walked on, feeling happy about the destiny of my bread, until the man started screaming at me.

Flailing his arms, he flung the box into the middle of the chess gathering. The dialogue that ensued is too profane to print, but I think the general idea was that he didn't like me or want my bread. He was insulted by it, and I seemed to be a highly undesirable person for giving it to him.

I scurried along while some of the chess players tried to shut him up. I guess they'd seen displays like this before.

Back in my hotel room, it occurred to me that I'd just seen a good analogy for the cross. God gave the world the Bread of Life but He wasn't what they wanted. They didn't recognize how special He was, and they discarded Him in anger. Yet the whole world starves for His love.

What are you craving today? Whatever the need is, the answer is Jesus.

Okra Epiphanies

And behold, the LORD passed by, and a great and strong wind tore into the mountains and broke the rocks in pieces before the LORD, but the LORD was not in the wind; and after the wind an earthquake, but the LORD was not in the earthquake; and after the earthquake a fire, but the LORD was not in the fire; and after the fire a still small voice.

1 KINGS 19:11–12 NKJV

I like to talk to my friend Dena when I'm feeling crazy. Dena has three little girls, and like me she gets these urges of wanting to give them perfect childhood experiences that are spiritual, educational, healthy, and fun. We constantly cook up plans of this sort that sometimes work out and sometimes don't...like the summer Dena decided she and her girls would have the lovely, back-to-nature experience of a vegetable garden.

Some of their vegetables turned out beautifully; her okra was extremely prolific. For a few weeks, every time I saw Dena she was dealing with okra—bagging it, giving it away, even surreptitiously putting it in dishes like cornbread she hoped her girls would eat.

One day Dena told me she'd had an epiphany in the vegetable garden: "I had scissors in my pocket to cut the okra. The girls wanted to use them, so I handed them the scissors and told them to take turns. I really wasn't paying much attention, because I was watching the ground for snakes. There were lots of weeds, and I was terrified one might be hiding in there, waiting to bite us. When I looked up, the girls were fighting over the scissors. I grabbed them back, and then it dawned on me: I was so focused on a distant, unknown danger that I failed to see the danger right before my eyes—the one I had brought in my own pocket."

Some time later she related another okra epiphany: "You know, Gwen, I'd been cutting the okra all this time, either with a knife or scissors. One day I forgot to bring anything but reached in and tried to break off some by hand. It just pops right off! You don't even have to use scissors. If you break it right where it attaches, it just snaps off in your hand."

She continued thoughtfully. "Isn't that just like life sometimes? We think we have to do things the hard way when, really, there's a simple design—a solution right before our eyes—if we'd just open them and look."

Yep. I can relate to that. It's good to be reminded, and it's good to know that God can speak to us in the okra patch. Some people might think that's crazy, but I think it's cool.

Suggestion for the day: listen for the voice of God everywhere, even in places you might not imagine He'd speak.

A Tale of Two Curtains

The sun stopped shining. And the curtain of the
temple was torn in two. Jesus called out with a loud
voice, "Father, into your hands I commit My spirit."
When he had said this, he breathed his last.

LUKE 23:45–46 NIV

I got an education when I went to Jerusalem. I met
a Palestinian kid who sold Star of David pendants;
I ate very interesting food; and I fell into a sort of awed
reverence as I walked the Via Dolorosa. But what I
remember most is standing in front of the Wailing Wall.

It's not because the Hasidic Jews were so interesting with their chanting, rocking, curls, and Old
Testaments, even though they were. And it's not
because there were women *literally* wailing beside me.
It's because of the cracks and crags in the ancient wall
of Solomon's temple where thousands of little rolled-
up papers rest.

Prayers, I found out when I asked. People bring them from all over the world. There are even services in Jerusalem that will print off prayers and stuff them in the wall after the requests are e-mailed to them. When the cracks get too crowded, somebody removes the papers and the process starts over again with new ones. It's an astonishing phenomenon.

It seems there are people who believe that their prayers have a better chance of being answered if they are stuck in the temple wall. Like a Jewish version of Lourdes, the wall represents a sacred presence—a place infused with holy meaning because of something that happened there or because the presence of God used to reside near there in the Holy of Holies.

When I learned about this practice I had a moment of existential crisis. It was one of those moments when you look at yourself and you look at the world and you see the other in a way you've never seen it before, and instead of feeling connected to others as a part of the collective human experience, you realize how different and far apart and alone we can be in our beliefs about reality.

In this case, reality all comes down to one's choice of curtains. As a believer in Jesus I have no concept of sticking prayers in walls. His death on the cross tore my curtain—the one that separated me and God—in two. That means I can talk to God about everything and He listens and answers; and while that's a very sacred, holy thing, it's also familiar, comfortable, and easy.

I respect the people who give prayers to be stuffed. I respect their needs and sympathize with the cries of their hearts. What I wish is that somehow I could let them know it doesn't have to be so hard. We don't have to approach God from behind a curtain, striving to be heard through a barrier. God isn't that distant, because Jesus tore the curtain in two.

Close your eyes and breathe in. He's like the air around you, as close as your nearest breath. Enjoy that nearness today.

Conclusion—
for the Days Ahead...

He has made everything beautiful.

ECCLESIASTES 3:11 NKJV

The other day I was driving my truck home from the university. The sun was shining, and as it radiated beams of light through the canopy of trees overhanging the road, I felt happy. My classes had gone well. I was looking forward to picking up Adelaide at my parents', being in my clean house, making a yummy dinner, and seeing my big kids and husband when they came home. I rolled down the windows, felt the breeze in my hair, and cranked up "A Beautiful Day" by U2: "The heart is a bloom...shoots up through the stony ground." I love that song.

The next day it was raining. When we got in the truck that morning, I saw that our goat was out, eating some new muscadine plants we'd just bought. They weren't even in the ground yet! I had to try to put him back in his pen before taking the kids to school, which was a muddy job that made us late.

The kids fussed in the car as I sped down the road. I turned on the radio and heard about a bloody attack on soldiers in Baghdad and brutality toward women in Afghanistan. The cell phone rang, and my mom told me that someone precious to me was in the hospital, fighting for his life. "Just thought you'd want to know, so you could pray," she said.

As I drove myself and my youngest home after dropping off the other two, I thought about the contrast of the second morning from the day before and how things really can turn on a dime. Chris Coppernoll writes in his novel *Screen Play* that our lives are a spin on the Potter's wheel. Sometimes that's a soft, gentle ride, and other times it whirls so fast it can make us sick. No irony was lost on me when I switched from the radio to the CD player and "A Beautiful Day" was still playing: "See the bird with the leaf in her mouth...after the flood all the colors came out...it's a beautiful day...don't let it get away."

One of the great things about writing a book like this

is that I got to immerse myself in beautiful stories. I pondered the mystery of God's beauty, and I celebrated beautiful days in my own life and the lives of others. I came alive to the truth that, in Him, the simplest days really are beautiful, that He's there on the ugly ones, too, and that He does return beauty for ashes. And then I got the chance to practice what I preached.

I want everyone who reads this book to know that for me, just as for anyone else, a beautiful day is a choice. It's a decision we make every day—and moment by moment throughout the day—to trust that God is here. Our Emmanuel, He climbed inside human flesh and *dwelt among us*, with all of our weaknesses and all of our warts. It is Him that makes everything beautiful. He is still with us, in our best moments as well as in our ugly ones. And He always will be.

Have a beautiful day!

Gwen Ford Faulkenberry lives and writes in the mountains of Ozark, Arkansas. Her passion is Jesus and the family He has given her. She likes to dance with her husband, Stone; catch fish with Harper (8); practice guitar with Grace (10); and read books with Adelaide (4). Gwen also holds a master's degree in liberal arts and enjoys teaching literature at a local university, raising goats and chickens, and playing the piano at her church. Gwen is the author of two novels, *Love Finds You in Romeo, Colorado,* and *Love Finds You in Branson, Missouri,* and three devotionals for women: *A Beautiful Life,* *A Beautiful Day,* and *Jesus, Be Near Me.* She loves to hear from her readers and share in the beauty of their stories. Drop her an e-mail at gfaulkenberry@hotmail.com.